the true book of

INDIANS

By Teri Martini

All children love to read about Indians before the settlers came to this country.

The mother Indians, the fathers, the children, the Indians that were alike in so many ways, but who lived their lives so differently

Here in pictures and simple text, are the Indians of the seacoast, the plains, the deserts, the swamps and the woodlands, their ways of living controlled by their environment.

A bright factual book for beginning readers.

the true book of

Indians

By Teri Martini

Illustrated by Charles Heston

 CHILDRENS PRESS, CHICAGO

The "true book" series is
prepared under the direction of
Illa Podendorf
Laboratory School, University of Chicago

Ninety-eight per cent of the text is in words from
the Combined Word List for Primary Reading.

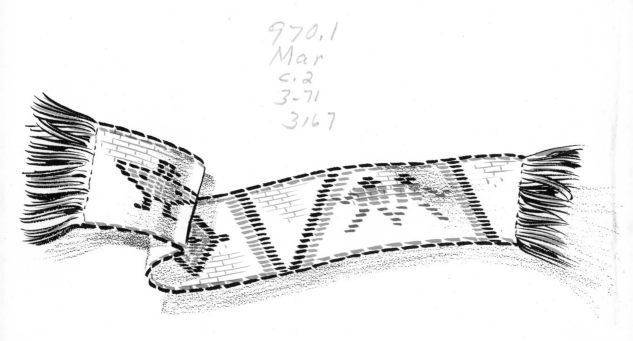

In the Beginning...

Long ago there was a land bridge between what is now Russia and Alaska. Hunters followed herds of wild animals across this land into North America.

As years went by, these hunters moved south and east across the country. They followed the animals and ate the wild plants they found.

Thousands of years later Columbus discovered the New World. He thought he had reached India, so he called the people Indians. We still call them Indians—American Indians.

These Indians lived in groups we call tribes. Some of the tribes settled in places where there were plenty of animals to be hunted. Others moved into parts of the country where there was land that was easily farmed. They soon learned to grow food. Still others stayed near the coast where the fishing was good.

Because they settled in very different kinds of places, the Indians lived quite differently. They ate different kinds of food. They built different kinds of houses for shelter. They also made different kinds of clothes and had different customs.

Indians of the Northwest Coast

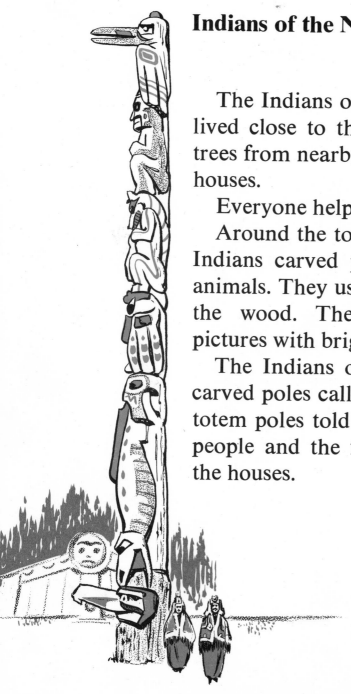

The Indians of the Northwest Coast lived close to the sea. They used the trees from nearby forests to build their houses.

Everyone helped.

Around the tops of the houses these Indians carved pictures of birds and animals. They used sharp stones to cut the wood. Then they painted the pictures with bright colors.

The Indians of the Northwest also carved poles called totem poles. These totem poles told the stories of famous people and the families who lived in the houses.

These Indians discovered many ways to catch fish in the rivers and in the sea.

The Indian men made canoes from logs. They would fish from the shore and from canoes. The Indian boys helped them.

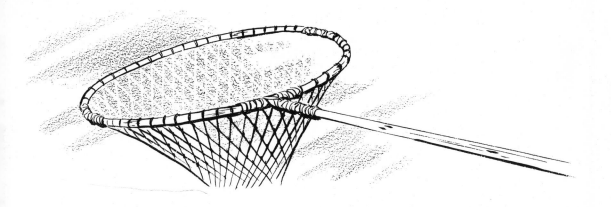

Most of the time the Indians fished in the rivers. Some of the men and boys would fish from the shore. Others would fish from small canoes. The Indians used spears and nets to catch the fish in the rivers. They could catch many fish this way.

Sometimes the Indian fishermen went out on the sea. Then they used their big canoes. In each canoe there would be many men.

These Indians were brave and strong. They would paddle far out to sea to hunt for giant whales. They took their harpoons with them.

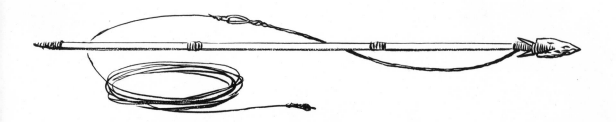

The strongest men threw harpoons at the whale. Swish! Away the whale would go, pulling the canoe through the water. It was very exciting and very dangerous. The whale could swim for a long time, even with the harpoons in it.

At last the whale would stop. The Indians had killed it. How happy they were. Here was food for many people for many days. The people in the village would be pleased to see how well the fishermen had done.

Everybody helped to cut up the whale. All the people in the tribe would get some meat. The meat would last a long time.

The Indian women and the little girls cleaned the meat with sharp shells. Then they cooked some of the meat in wooden pots. This part the Indians would eat right away.

The rest of the meat was hung over the fire until the smoke dried it. The Indians put this smoked meat into wooden boxes. They would use it during the long winter when food was hard to get.

In the winter the Indian women wove skirts and hats out of dried grass and the bark of trees. The little girls helped, too.

The women also made warm robes for the men from the skins of animals. They used wool from the dogs to make blankets. They wove mats for rugs and baskets in which to carry fish.

The Indians who lived on the Northwest Coast had giveaway parties. The person who had the party gave away many things. He would do this to show how rich he was. At these parties, everyone in the village was fed. This way the Indians who were poor got food and gifts.

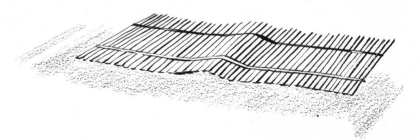

A giveaway party was called a POTLATCH. At these parties there was always singing and dancing. The boys and girls would have races up and down the sand. Everyone had a good time.

Indians of the Plains

Another group of Indians settled near the Great Plains. Herds of buffalo thundered across this grassy, treeless land. For thousands of years these Indians hunted the buffalo on foot because they had no horses.

Then the Spanish explorers brought horses to North America. When the Indians got some of the horses, their way of life changed. They soon became expert horsemen. Some of them moved onto the Plains. They became dependent upon the buffalo for food, for clothing, and for many other things.

Other Indians planted corn in the spring and then moved to the Plains to hunt buffalo during the summer. In the fall they would return home for the harvest.

The Indian men were brave hunters. They would ride their horses through the buffalo herd and kill the buffalo with bows and arrows.

How busy the Indian women were after a buffalo hunt! The Plains Indians used almost every part of the buffalo for something.

The wool from the head was used to make blankets. The hide was used to make robes for the winter and for moccasin soles. The bones made

fine sharp tools. The horns were often used as ornaments for headdresses.

The Indian women scraped the hair from the skins and sewed them together to make tepees.

Many of the Plains Indians lived almost entirely on buffalo meat. The meat that was not eaten right away was cut in strips and smoked over a fire. Some of this meat was ground and mixed with grease and with dried berries. This kind of food was called PEMMICAN.

Pemmican could be stored for a long time. It could be used in the winter when it was hard to find fresh food.

When the buffalo moved, the Plains Indians would move, too. They would pack up all their things, even their tepees. They put their goods on a wooden frame called a TRAVOIS. Horses or dogs would pull the travois. The whole tribe would follow the buffalo across the Plains.

The Indian women made clothes from the skins of elk and deer. They sewed the skins with bone needles. Then they painted colored bands on the clothes. Sometimes they would trim the clothes with beads and porcupine quills.

During the winter, the heavy buffalo robes helped to keep the Indians warm. In the summer the men and boys wore very little clothing.

The Indian women cooked, made clothes, and took care of the children. The Indian men spent most of their time hunting and fighting.

A Plains Indian warrior painted his face with colored clay. Each tribe had its own face-paint designs.

Indian braves used spears, and bows and arrows. The spearheads and arrowheads were made of bone or flint. The heads were fastened to the shaft with leather thongs. The arrows used by the Plains Indians had short shafts with long feathers. Every warrior carried a shield.

The bravest Indians could wear bonnets with many eagle feathers. Eagle feathers were given as an award for bravery.

The Plains Indians usually fought for personal glory or revenge. They thought of war as a game. The important thing for an Indian warrior was to show personal bravery.

The Plains Indians spoke different languages. When Indians from different tribes met, they talked with their hands. This was sign language.

When Indians wanted to send messages over a long distance, they used smoke signals. To make smoke signals, they would hold a blanket over a fire. When they took the blanket off, a puff of smoke rose into the sky. Smoke puffs could be seen from many miles away. The number of smoke puffs and the time in between the puffs had special meanings.

RIGHT HERE   ELK   I SEE

Indians of the Southwest

Some Indian tribes settled in the Southwest. Here there was little rain. The days were very hot and the nights were cool.

This was desert land, but there were a few rivers and streams. The Indians built their houses near a river or stream whenever they could. They

were farmers. They needed the water for their crops as well as for drinking.

These Indians used clay mixed with stones and grass to make bricks. This kind of building material is called ADOBE. With these adobe bricks, the Indians built houses four and five stories high. Wooden ladders led from one level to the next.

A house of this kind is called a PUEBLO. This is a Spanish word meaning village. The Spanish called these people Pueblo Indians.

Pueblo Indians grew corn, beans, and squash in their gardens. It was hard to grow things in this dry country. The Indians had to carry water from the streams to their gardens. Some tribes dug ditches to carry the water from the rivers to their crops.

These Indians used very simple farming tools. They had pointed sticks which were used for digging. They had hoes made of wood or bone.

Among the Pueblo Indians the man was the farmer. But women and children also worked in

the fields when they were needed. Raising crops in this dry land was hard work.

When the corn was harvested, it was put on the flat roof to dry. Squash and beans were also dried. The dried food could be kept for a long time. This meant that there would be food to eat during times when there was no rain.

The Indian women spent many hours grinding corn between stones. They made thin corn bread. They also made corn dumplings and corn stew. They cooked most of the food in round, brick ovens.

The Pueblo Indians were happy when it rained on their gardens. Rain was important to these farmers. Without rain, the crops would die. Then there would not be much food. Many people would go hungry.

When there was no rain, the Indians had to use water from a nearby river. Sometimes they built ditches to carry the water. If there were no ditches, the water had to be carried from the river in jars. This was hard work. Even then, the crops might not get enough water.

The Pueblo Indians did not know what made it rain. They thought that there were strange people living under the ground. These people could do almost anything.

One tribe of Pueblo Indians, the Hopi, did a snake dance to bring rain. This dance was held in August. It would last for nine days. Certain Indians, called Snake priests, would dance with live snakes in their mouths. At the end of the dance the snakes were put out on the desert. The Indians thought the snakes went back to tell the underground people to send rain.

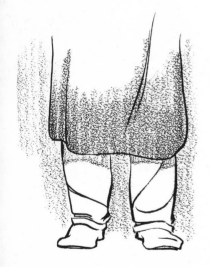

Pueblo women found wild cotton growing in the desert. They wove this cotton into cloth. The Pueblo Indians were good weavers. In some tribes the men did the weaving.

The cotton cloth was used to make dresses, skirts, and shirts. The edges of the clothes were trimmed with colored threads.

Everyone wore leather boots to protect their feet from the sharp rocks and rough grasses on the ground.

The women made clay jars to carry water. They also made clay jars in which to store food. Even the little girls learned to carry these jars on their heads while climbing the wooden ladders.

When the boys and girls weren't busy helping, they liked to play. Among the Pueblo Indians, footraces were most popular.

Indians of the Southeast

Some Indians traveled into the Southeast. Here there were many rivers and much rain. It was a good place to grow corn, beans, and other vegetables.

But settlers came. They wanted the good land, too. They chased many Indians into damp land called SWAMPS. The Indians who stayed in the swamps were the Seminoles.

This was a beautiful, green land with tall trees and green grasses. Most beautiful of all were the many colored birds that lived there. There were blue, yellow, red, and pink birds.

It was hard to grow crops where water stayed on the ground and made it damp. But the Indians learned to live on the wild plants and animals they found there.

The ground was so damp that the Seminole Indians built their houses on posts. The roofs were made of wood and covered with palm leaves. It was so hot that the houses had no walls.

While the Seminoles went about their work, they wore little clothing. They hunted deer and wild turkeys with bows and arrows.

They took care of their vegetable gardens. They fished in the streams and lakes. They knew how to use nets and spears.

They even knew how to catch fish with their hands.

Sometimes they hunted the pretty birds with blowguns. They blew a sharp piece of cane through a long hollow pole. This dart killed the bird, but did not spoil the feathers. The Seminole Indians did not want to spoil the feathers because they liked to wear them.

These Indians liked to play ball games. In one of these games, each player carried a long stick with a net on the end. They threw the ball back and forth and caught it in this net. The players wore tails of different animals for good luck.

Indians of the Northeast Woodlands

Some Indian tribes settled in the Northeast Woodlands. Here they lived by hunting, fishing, trapping, and farming. They built light canoes out of birchbark with which to travel over the many lakes and rivers.

These Indians hunted deer in the forests with bows and arrows. They fished in the lakes and rivers with nets and spears. In their gardens they grew corn, beans, pumpkins, and sweet potatoes. The women also gathered grapes, nuts, and berries which grew wild.

The Indian women were good cooks. Most of the time they cooked meat by broiling or roasting it. But sometimes they would boil the meat. To do this, they would fill a jar with water. Then they put in the meat. After that they dropped in hot stones. This made the water boil and cook the meat.

Many of the Eastern Woodland Indians made a corn cake called HOMINY. To make hominy, they would soak grains of corn in wood ashes and water. This made the kernels puff up. Then the skins would soak off and float to the top. The kernels were then ready to be washed and cooked.

The Indians of the Northeast made their houses out of logs and tree bark.

The Iroquois Indians lived in a large log building called a LONGHOUSE. There was a long hall through the middle. There were rooms on either side. Twenty families could live in one longhouse.

The Delaware Indians lived in round, one-room houses called WIGWAMS. These were made by bending saplings and covering them with bark.

In the summer the men and boys wore only breechcloths and moccasins. In winter they wore leggings and shirts of deerskin.

The women and girls wore short skirts. They had robes of skins and fur for winter. They often wore earrings and necklaces made of animals' teeth.

In winter the ground was often covered with deep snow. Then the Eastern Woodland Indians made SNOWSHOES to help them walk over the snow. They made snowshoes by lacing strips of leather across a wooden frame. The Indians tied the snowshoes to their feet with other pieces of leather.

The Eastern Woodland Indians liked to be strong and healthy.

Every spring and fall certain men, called medicine men, put on masks or false faces. Then they would go from house to house. They sang loudly. They shook turtle-shell rattles. They thought they were chasing away the evil spirits who caused sickness.

In the spring, the Indians would tap the maple trees. They would drink the sap as a tonic.

The Eastern Woodland Indians made strings of beads called WAMPUM. Wampum is a name for beads made from shells. These beads were white or purple or black. The Indians would make the wampum into belts or sew it on their clothing.

The white beads meant peace or health. The dark beads meant war or death. The Indians also made pictures with the beads. The pictures told a story of their people or were a record of treaties.

After the settlers came, the strings of wampum were used as money. Wampum belts were also given to the settlers as a sign of friendship.

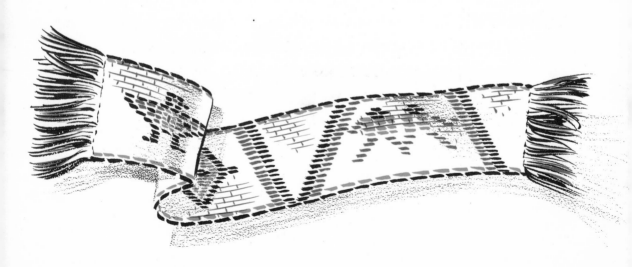

Over thousands of years the Indians slowly spread across the country, from north to south and west to east. Finally, Indians were working and playing in all parts of the land. Some lived by the sea, on the Northwest Coast. Some lived in the Southwest part of the country. Others lived on the Great Plains between the Rocky Mountains and the Mississippi River. Some lived in the swamps in the Southeast. Still others lived in the Northeastern Woodlands.

Each group of Indians lived in a different way. How each group lived depended upon the part of the country in which it settled. Each group lived in a different kind of house. Each ate different kinds of food. Each wore different kinds of clothes. Each had different customs. But all these Indians learned to use wisely whatever was found in that part of the land in which they made their home.